Superstars
of the
PITTSBURGH
STEELERS

by M. J. Cosson

AMICUS HIGH INTEREST   AMICUS INK

Amicus High Interest and
Amicus Ink are imprints of Amicus
P.O. Box 1329, Mankato, MN 56002
www.amicuspublishing.us

Library of Congress Cataloging-in-Publication Data
Cosson, M. J.
  Superstars of the Pittsburgh Steelers / M.J. Cosson.
     pages cm. -- (Pro sports superstars)
  ISBN 978-1-60753-529-4 (hardcover) -- ISBN 978-1-60753-559-1 (eBook)
  ISBN 978-1-68152-066-7 (paperback)
  1. Pittsburgh Steelers (Football team)--History--Juvenile literature.
2. Football players--United States--Biography--Juvenile literature. I. Title.
  GV956.P57C67 2014
  796.332'640974886--dc23
                          2013006507

Photo Credits: Tom DiPace/AP Images, cover, 2, 14, 21, 22; Mike Fabus/AP
Images, 5; NFL Photos/AP Images, 6, 10, 13; AP Images, 9; Gene J. Puskar/
AP Images, 17; Mike Groll/AP Images, 18

Produced for Amicus by The Peterson Publishing Company
and Red Line Editorial.

Editor: Jenna Gleisner
Designer: Becky Daum

Printed in Malaysia

HC 10 9 8 7 6 5 4
PB 10 9 8 7 6 5 4 3 2 1

TABLE OF CONTENTS

MEET THE PITTSBURGH STEELERS

The Pittsburgh Steelers have made it to eight Super Bowls. They won six of them. That is more than any other team. The Steelers are super tough. Here are some of their best players.

JOE GREENE

Joe Greene played **defense**. He was fast. He used his strength to tackle. He played in four Super Bowls. He helped win all four. He went to ten **Pro Bowls**. His first one was in 1970.

"Mean" Joe Greene got his nickname in college. His college team was called the "Mean Green."

TERRY BRADSHAW

Terry Bradshaw was an amazing **quarterback.** He had a strong arm. He threw for 212 touchdowns. He helped the Steelers win four Super Bowls.

Bradshaw was the NFL MVP in 1978.

FRANCO HARRIS

Franco Harris was a powerful runner. The Steelers won the 1974 Super Bowl. They played the Minnesota Vikings. Harris rushed for 158 yards. He also scored a touchdown. He was the MVP.

JACK LAMBERT

Jack Lambert played tough. He won an award for playing defense in 1976. He played in nine Pro Bowls in a row. He helped the Steelers win four Super Bowls.

JEROME BETTIS

Jerome Bettis was great at running with the ball. He played **offense**. His last game was the Super Bowl in 2006. The Steelers won.

Bettis was called "The Bus" because he was big. He ran with great force.

HINES WARD

Hines Ward was quick. He was crafty. He went to four Pro Bowls. He helped win two Super Bowls. He was the Super Bowl MVP in 2006. He holds many records.

TROY POLAMALU

Troy Polamalu is a tough **tackler**.
He was named to the NFL's
All-Decade team for the 2000s.
He has helped win two Super
Bowls. He has been picked to play
in seven Pro Bowls.

Polamalu's long hair makes him easy to spot on the field.

BEN ROETHLISBERGER

Ben Roethlisberger has a strong arm. He was a **rookie** in 2004. He led the Steelers to the Super Bowl three times. He helped win two of them. He is the youngest quarterback to win a Super Bowl.

The Steelers have had many great stars. Who will be the next?

TEAM FAST FACTS

Founded: 1933

Other Names: Pittsburgh Pirates (1933–1939)

Nicknames: Black and Gold, Men of Steel

Home Stadium: Heinz Stadium (Pittsburgh, Pennsylvania)

Super Bowl Titles: 6 (1974, 1975, 1978, 1979, 2005, and 2008)

Hall of Fame Players: 16, including Joe Greene, Terry Bradshaw, and Jack Lambert

WORDS TO KNOW

defense – the group of players that tries to stop the other team from scoring

MVP – Most Valuable Player; an honor given to the best player each season

NFL – National Football League; the league pro football players play in

offense – the group of players that tries to score

Pro Bowl – the NFL's all-star game

quarterback – a player whose main jobs are to lead the offense and throw passes

rookie – a player in his first season

tackler – a player whose main job is knocking players on the other team to the ground so they cannot score

LEARN MORE

Books

Frisch, Aaron. *Pittsburgh Steelers*. Mankato, MN: Creative Education, 2011.

LeBoutillier, Nate. *Pittsburgh Steelers*. Mankato, MN: Creative Education, 2006.

Web Sites

NFL.com
http://nfl.com
Check out pictures and your favorite football players' stats.

NFL Rush
http://www.nflrush.com
Play games and learn how to be a part of NFL PLAY 60.

Steelers Kids Zone
http://www.steelers.com/community/kids-zone.html
Learn more about the Pittsburgh Steelers.

INDEX